Lunch at the Calories-Don't-Count Café

Lunch at the Calories-Don't-Count Café

Susan Sturgill

Susan Sturgill
8/2/98

The Laughing Academy Press
P.O. Box 82061 • Columbus OH 43202

ISBN 0-9626108-5-2

Manufactured in the U.S.A. Printed and bound by Worzalla Publishing Co., Stevens Point WI, for The Laughing Academy Press in a first edition of 2500 copies October 6, 1995.

There is no love sincerer than
the love of food.
— George Bernard Shaw

Calories don't count if it's not in the book

... calories couldn't possibly count if they're frozen;

and calories don't count if you're cold

Other useful dates: Canada Day: July 1; the
Queen Mother's birthday Aug. 4; Respect for the Aged Day in Japan
Sept. 15; Cinco de Mayo; Federal Fiscal New Year's Day Oct. 1.

Calories don't count if nobody sees you.

Calories don't count in the interests of science

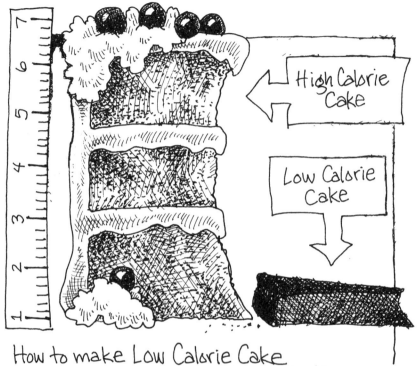

High Calorie
Cake

Low Calorie
Cake

How to make Low Calorie Cake
Melt 10oz. semisweet chocolate with ½c. butter.
Beat 6 egg yolks, gradually adding ¾c. granulated
sugar. Add chocolate mixture, 2 tsp. créme de cacao,

and ½ tsp. vanilla. Beat six egg whites until soft peaks form. Beat in ¼ c. granulated sugar to stiff peak stage. Fold whites into chocolate mixture.

Pour batter into buttered and floured springform pan. Bake 15 min. at 375°, 15 min. at 350°, 30 min. at 250°. Turn off oven and leave cake in with door propped open for 30 minutes.

Cake top will collapse. Press down lightly to smooth top. Serve at room temp. with whipped cream.

Wow, those are the lowest calories I've ever seen

Never apologize. Never explain.
Never look back.